ETHICAL HACKING

A Comprehensive Beginner's Guide to Learn and Master Ethical Hacking

TABLE OF CONTENTS

Introduction

Congratulations on purchasing *Ethical Hacking: A Comprehensive Beginner's Guide to Learn and Master Ethical Hacking* and thank you for doing so. It doesn't matter if you are a computer security professional ready to take the next step or someone interested in the how-to of hacking, this book is for you. With the information inside, you'll learn everything you need to know to start hacking tomorrow.

The following chapters discuss ethical hacking in both general and technical terms. You will learn about terminology, enumeration, sniffing, system hacking, social engineering, malware, denial of service attacks, honeypots, and more. You will learn about the variety of tools that ethical hackers use as well as the processes they are used for. This book walks you through the ins-and-outs of hacking, from the basic ideas to complex technical processes. You will learn about everything you need to know to get started.

Prerequisite

This book assumes you have a general understanding of computers and networking. Also important to know about operating systems and command line prompts. However, if you are just starting out, this book is still for you. Throughout this book, you will learn the basics to build off of and master the skills you need.

There are plenty of books on this subject on the market, thanks again for choosing this one! Every effort was made to ensure it is full of as much useful information as possible, please enjoy!

Chapter 1

What is Ethical Hacking?

What is Hacking?

Hacking is the art of computer intrusion, both with or without permission. Merriam-Webster dictionary defines hacker as "an expert at programming and solving problems with a computer" or "a person who illegally gains access to and sometimes tampers with information in a computer system." Hacking refers to manipulating weaknesses and bugs to infiltrate a computer network. Hackers exploit weaknesses to gain access to sensitive data, damage computer systems or gain bragging rights for the hack.

In the beginning, hacker was a positive word, but as cybercriminals began to hack for illicit purposes, the term took on a negative connotation. This negative interpretation is fueled by the media, which often depict hackers as evil, using their skills to commit illegal acts. Hence, most people think hackers are solely malicious, but there are many ethical hackers as well.

What is Ethical Hacking?

Ethical hacking is when hackers use their skills not to harm or damage the systems, but to test them for weaknesses or ways a system might be attacked to improve the overall security of the system. These hackers work hand-in-hand with companies to prevent damage, loss of sensitive data, and to prevent malicious intrusions. Ethical hackers gain permission from the companies they work for before the hack, with specific goals to accomplish, and use their skills to attack the system to expose weaknesses. This method is highly effective and used by companies and governments all over the world to keep their systems safe. In essence, ethical hackers are the good guys.

It is essential for an ethical hacker to gain permission from the appropriate management representative, convey the scope of the hack, determine if anything is off-limits (like sensitive customer data), and make sure the hack is legal. If the ethical hacker does not have the correct permission to do the security analysis, the ethical may still have legal repercussions.

It is also the responsibility of the white hat to write a report on their findings for the company to assist the organization in securing the system.

History of Hacking

Hacking goes back to the 1930s when cryptologists from Poland broke the code of the Enigma machine, a German cipher machine that sent encrypted morse code messages. This was followed in 1939 when the mathematician and logician Alan Turing, working at the Government Code and Cypher School (GC&CS) at Bletchley Park, created the Bombe machine that cracked German messages, giving the Allies reliable intelligence against the Nazis, which helped to end World War II. Turing went on to become the father of artificial intelligence and theoretical computer science.

In 1943, the punch card system used by the Nazis was hacked by René Carmille. The punch card system was used to identify Jews by the Nazi forces.

The term "hack" was first used at the Massachusetts Institute of Technology (MIT) in the 1950s, and it meant experimenting with computers. The term originally was used by engineering students to make various systems more efficient. It was first used by the Tech Model Railroad Club (TMRC) and the MIT Artificial Intelligence Laboratory. This early hacking was benign. The original intent of these hackers was playful and more about curiosity about how computer systems worked and how the systems could be manipulated. This led to a continuing series of pranks at MIT, which continues today, including turning the side of a building into a Tetris board, putting a mock police car on top of the Dome with the lights flashing, and installing Linux instead of Windows on a sign-in computer during Bill Gate's visit to the campus.

The 1970s saw the rise of the phreaker sub-culture. John Draper, also known as Captain Crunch, created the first "blue box" that imitates the tones used by telephone companies. Phreakers used blue boxes to make expensive long-distance calls for free or wiretap phones.

The 1980s were an important time for hacking. The term hacker went from mostly benign to malicious when it was associated with criminal intent. The first laws against hacking were established, and the media began depicting hackers are committing illicit acts. Blackhat hackers began to appear in science fiction and popular culture.

Below is a timeline of major events from the 1980s to today:

- 1981: the Chaos Computer Club was formed. It went on to become the largest European group of hackers.

- 1983: Ken Thompson introduced the idea of a trojan horse.

- 1983: The film *Wargames* was released. The movie depicts a hacker gaining access to a NORAD supercomputer that runs simulations of nuclear war, and by an accident almost causes World War III. The film caused a scare among the public.

- 1984: William Gibson published *Neuromancer*, a science fiction story belonging to the Cyberpunk genre, which depicts the hacker Case. It introduces several terms including ICE, matrix, cyberspace, and simstim.

- 1985: The Secret Service, FBI, Middlesex County New Jersey Prosecutors, and various local law enforcement seized equipment from operators of various Bulletin Board Systems

(BBS) boards. This event is referred to as the Private Sector Bust or the 2600 BBS Seizure.

- 1986: Loyd Blankenship, aka the Mentor, released the Hacker Manifesto on the ezine Phrack.

- 1986: the Computer Fraud and Abuse Act is passed into law. The legislation made it illegal to hack into computer systems.

- 1988: Robert T. Morris Jr launched the Morris Worm, which infected 6,000 computers, including many university and government systems. Also in 1988, the First National Bank of Chicago is hacked resulting in a $70 million theft. Kevin Poulson, also known as Dark Dante, goes into hiding after hacking a federal computer network.

- 1989: Robert Morris is convicted under the Computer Fraud and Abuse Act. He was the first person convicted under the new law.

- 1991: Kevin Poulsen is arrested and sentenced to 5 years in prison.

- 1992: Kevin Mitnick breaks probation and begins to hack in earnest. He is arrested after two and a half years and sentenced to over 5 years in prison.

- 1994: Vladimir Levin hacks Citibank and steals $10,000,000. Levin is arrested in 1995 and sentenced to 3 years in prison.

- 1995: John Patrick, Vice President of IBM, coins the term ethical hacking.

- 1997: The AOHELL malware disrupts America Online (AOL), causing damage to email and chat boards.

- 2000: The ILOVEYOU worm spreads by email resulting in $10 billion in damages. Michael "MafiaBoy" Calce uses distributed denial of service (DDoS) attacks to take down eBay, CNN,

Dell.com, and Yahoo!. This happens over the course of a week. In 2001 he is arrested for bragging about his DDoS attack and is sentenced to open custody.

- 2002: Gary "Solo" McKinnon hacks US military computers. The US requests extradition. In 2013 Teresa May blocks the extradition.

- 2004: Jason Smothers sells the details of AOL customers to spammers. 92 million customers' data is sold. Smothers was sent to prison for a year.

- 2007: George Holz jailbreaks the first iPhone, unlocking it for use with any carrier. In 2010 he cracks the PlayStation 3.

- 2008: The Chaos Culture Club protests the German use of biometric data. They release the German Minister of the Interior's fingerprints to the public.

- 2010: The Stuxnet worm is released. It deals damage to an Iranian nuclear site. There is damage to both the equipment and to the computer systems. Barnaby Jack demonstrates an ATM hack that causes an ATM to spit out money.

- 2011: LulzSec, a hacker collective, hacks Sony several times. The group steals information on millions of users. In 2011 Barnaby Jack hacks an insulin pump.

- 2012: 1.5 million customers have their credit card numbers stolen when MasterCard and Visa are hacked.

- 2013: Anonymous, a hacker group, hacked the North Korean government's Twitter and Flickr accounts. In 2015, following the Charlie Hebdo shootings in Paris, Anonymous began a campaign against the Islamic State, disrupting their communications, doing disturbed denial of service attacks, and installing malware on the IS website and devices that connect to it.

- 2014: Sony Entertainment is hacked over the movie the Interview, which made North Korea's leader Kim Jong Un look bad. North Korean hackers are blamed for the attack.

- 2016: The US Presidential Election is hacked by the Russians. Russian hackers used botnets, placed ads on social media, and posted to Facebook groups to cause discord in the American public. This hack was very successful in polarizing American politics and society.

- 2017: Equifax, a US credit reporting agency, is hacked. 145.5 million customer's data is compromised.

- 2018: Tesla, an electric car manufacturer, was hacked, and the company's cloud computing sources were used to mine cryptocurrency.

Hacker Sub-Cultures

There are several hacker sub-cultures.

Ethical hackers, or white hats, are hackers that use their skills to detect bugs and vulnerabilities in systems to expose weaknesses. White hats work with companies to protect systems from intrusion. White hats work within the law, and they are the "good" guys.

Black hats, or crackers, are hackers that use their skills to cause damage, steal data including credit card numbers and other sensitive information, or gain bragging rights. The activities of black hats are generally illegal. Black hats are the "bad" guys.

Grey hats are hackers that blur the line between white and black hats. They tend to hack to troll or for fun. Grey hats both exploit and report bugs. Grey hats hackers typically do not hack for their own advantage, but for reputation and the thrill of the hack.

Red hats are hackers that are essentially white hats that work with government agencies to protect government systems.

Phreakers are hackers that use blue boxes to imitate the tones used by telephone companies to place free long distance calls or wiretap phones.

Script kiddies are hackers who use pre-written tools and do not have a deep understanding of the technical aspects of computers.

State hackers are hackers employed by a nation-state to commit cyber attacks on other nations. China, North Korea, Russia, and the US are known to have state hackers.

Hacktivists are hackers who use their skills for political, social, or religious statements. Their hacks are usually illegal and are often DDoS attacks against a website or service. For example, the hacking collective Anonymous disabled Twitter accounts belonging to ISIS, installed malware on Islamic State devices which tracked the movements of the user, and gaining access to all the messages and multimedia on the infected devices.

Famous Hackers

Gary McKinnon is known for hacking the US military including NASA, the Army, and the Air Force. McKinnon claims he hacked to discover evidence of antigravity technology, UFOs, and "free energy." The US attempted to extradite McKinnon, but Teresa May blocked it.

Johan Helgis, or Julf, did product development for Eunet International, the first Pan-European ISP. Helgis became known in the 1980s for creating an anonymous remailer. Currently, he is on the board of Technologia Incognita.

Johnathon James hacked a password on a NASA server where he obtained the source code for the International Space Station and other data. James was the first juvenile to serve time in prison for cybercrime. In 2008, James committed suicide.

Kevin Mitnick is a security consultant and ethical hacker. Mitnick is also an author and has appeared in several documentaries about hacking. He was the first hacker on the FBI Most Wanted list. From the 1970s to 1995 he operated as a black hat hacker until he was captured. He infiltrated several major systems including Sun Microsystems, Netcom, Nokia, and Motorola. Mitnick is often considered a grey hat hacker due to his past as a black hat.

Kevin Poulson hacked federal systems for information on wiretaps. He also took over phone lines for a Los Angeles station KIIS-FM to win a Porsche in a radio caller contest. He served a sentence of five years. Poulson is currently a journalist.

Linus Torvalds is the creator of the Linux operating system. Linux is a Unix-based OS that is open source. He holds honorary doctorates from the University of Helsinki and Stockholm University. He continues to work on the Linux kernel.

Mark Abene, also known as Phiber Optik, is a white hat hacker who drew attention during the 1980s and early 1990s. Abene was early to defend ethical hacking as legitimate computer security. His clients include First USA, UBS, American Express, and others.

Robert Morris is the hacker behind the Morris Worm, which slowed down government and university systems in 1998. Morris claimed that he had no intention of the worm escaping the lab. However, it affected over 6,000 systems. Morris was sentenced to three years in prison, 400 hours of community service, and a penalty of $10,500. Morris currently teaches at MIT.

Steve "Woz" Wozniak, the inventor of the Apple computer and co-creator of Apple, Inc, was a member of the phreaker sub-culture in the 1970s before he invented the Apple I. Woz continues to purchase and test many devices for usability and security, often criticizing Apple products.

Chapter 2

Terminology and The Command Line

Terminology

- Adware: Software that forces ads to display on a computer or a mobile device.

- Attack: An incident where access is gained or data is extracted.

- Back Door: A hidden way to gain entry into a system or software that bypasses network security.

Black Hat: A hacker who hacks predominately for personal gain, fame, or to deface a company. Black hats are the "bad guys."

- Bot: An automated program that can do something repeatedly at a fast rate.

- Botnet: Multiple computers that are controlled without permission that generally do automated tasks. Also referred to as a zombie army.

- Brute Force Attack: An automated attack that tries different logins and password combinations until access is granted.

- Buffer Overflow: Buffer overflow is when more data is written to a computer system than a buffer can hold.

- Clone Phishing: Modifying an email with a fake link in an attempt to extract personal information.

- Cracker: A black hat that modifies software to gain unintended features.

- Cryptojacking: An attack on cloud computing services to mine cryptocurrency.

- Cryptocurrency: A type of digital currency where there is a way to verify funds, generate currency, and transfer funds with the need of a central bank.

- Denial of Service Attack (DoS): An attempt to make resources of a system unavailable to legitimate users by overloading the computer system.

- Distributed Denial of Service Attack (DDoS): A Denial of Service attack that comes from several computers at once. This is usually achieved with a botnet.

- Exploit Kit: The software that runs on web servers to identify vulnerabilities in client machines. It exploits vulnerabilities to install and run malicious code or malware.

- Exploit: An exploit is software or data that takes advantage of a bug or vulnerability.

- Firewall: A filter designed to protect against intruders while allowing communication between the systems behind the firewall and the internet.

Grey Hat: A hacker who blurs the line between white hat and black hat. A grey hat can hack either to help protect or to attack a system maliciously.

Hacktivist: Someone who hacks for political, social, or religious reasons.

- Keystroke Logger: Software that records keystrokes, which is the keys that are pushed on a keyboard or the places touched on a touchscreen. Often used to record logins and passwords.

- Logic Bomb: A virus that delivers a malicious action when some conditions are met.

- Malware: A group of malicious software that includes adware, ransomware, viruses, trojan horses, worms, etc.

- Master Program: A master program is a software that controls infected computers to send out spam or Denial of Service attacks.

- Phishing: An email fraud technique where the hacker sends out official looking emails to gather personal information like passwords, logins, credit card numbers, and other personal data.

- Phreaker: One of the original hacker sub-cultures that revolved around using blue boxes to make expensive long distance calls for free or to tap phones.

Risk: The chance for a threat to take advantage of a vulnerability.

Rootkit: Generally malicious software that hides processes and programs from detection and enables privileged access to the device.

Shrink Wrap Code: An attack that exploits unpatched software.

Social Engineering: An attempt to deceive to gain personal information.

Spam: Unwanted emails sent to a large number of people without the recipient's permission.

Spoofing: Attempt to gain access to a computer by sending a message that appears to come from a trusted host.

Spyware: Software that collects information about the user without permission. It may transfer that information to another computer or take control of the computer.

SQL Injection: An attack where SQL code is injected into entry fields to gain access, data, or install malware.

Trojan: A program that appears valid but that destroys files and alters or steals information.

Threat: A hacker or software that can exploit a vulnerability.

Virus: Code that replicates itself inside a computer and damages data or corrupts the computer system.

Vulnerability: A weakness in a computer system that can be exploited.

White Hat: A white hat is an ethical hacker who hacks to find exploits, bugs, and vulnerabilities to better protect computer systems. White hats are the "good guys."

Worm: A type of virus that self-replicates in active memory.

Cross-Site Scripting (XSS): A type of vulnerability in web applications that allows attackers to inject code into websites.

Zombie Drone: A computer that is unknowingly controlled by another computer without the user's knowledge. A zombie drone is also known as a soldier or a drone.

Command Line Prompts

Ethical hacking uses many tools, and command line prompts (CLP) are one of them. It is important to have a working knowledge of CLPs, as many of the tools use CLPs to operate them. Here are some helpful CLPs that come in handy while hacking.

Ping

Ping is a command that allows the user to determine TCP/IP, IP addresses, and networks.

Ping x.x.x.x (replace x with an IP address) or "ping www.example.com". Either syntax will run a ping on the server and respond with data about the ping.

nslookup

nslookup is a command used to query the domain name server (DNS) to obtain the IP address or domain name.

nslookup www.example.com

To find out the IP address of specific Mail Servers with nslookup use the following code:

NSLOOKUP (Press Enter)

SET TYPE=MX (Press Enter)

GOOGLE.COM/YAHOO.COM

tracert

tracert is a command line prompt that traces the route between the user's computer and a destination on the internet. This command also calculates the time each transfer takes.

tracert x.x.x.x (replace x with the IP address) or tracet www.google.com

arp

The arp command displays the arp table. This command helps locate arp poisoning.

ARP -A

Route

The route command displays the routing table, interface, metric, and gateway.

14

ROUTE PRINT

ipconfig

The ipconfig will display a lot of information such as the IP, Gateway, DNS, and other information.

IPCONFIG or IPCONFIG/ALL

To change a dynamic IP address use the following command:

IPCONFIG/RELEASE

IPCONFIG/RENEW

Netstat CMD

This command shows who has established connections with the computer and provide information on active connections and listing ports.

NETSTAT-A (Displays all connections)

METSTAT-N (Sorts the connections numerically)

NETSTAT-B (Displays executable)

Chapter 3

First Steps

The Process of Ethical Hacking

It is important for an ethical hacker to have a process to structure the hack. These processes can vary depending on the hacker and the companies desire.

Here is an example process to follow:

- Reconnaissance is the first step. Reconnaissance is when the ethical hacker gathers information about the target system.

- The next step is scanning the system. This includes scanning ports to find out which ones are open or closed.

- The next step is attacking the system. This is when the attacker gains access to the system. Metasploit is a useful tool in this phase (see Chapter 10).

- The next step is maintaining access to the target system. This generally is accomplished by installing backdoors.

- The next step is clearing your tracks. Essentially, this is deleting logs from the system and is considered unethical.

- Finally, there is reporting. This is the phase of preparing a report for the company the ethical hacker is working for.

What is Penetration Testing

Penetration testing, or pen-testing, is a term for IT security professionals to test a system to see how secure it is. While the process is very similar between a security professional and a white hat hacker, there are some differences in how detailed the pen-testing is versus an ethical hacker's attack.

Why Ethical Hacking

The main differences between a penetration test (pen-testing) or ethical hacking are that in pen-testing is smaller in scope. An ethical hacker tests the entire infrastructure and system while the IT professional tests just one area. The tester doesn't need extra permissions, and most any tester can perform the test. The tester generally only knows about the area of the network or system that the test is performed in. The ethical hacker, on the other hand, must be an expert in software, hardware, infrastructure, and have access to the entire network. The pen-tester does not need to write in-depth reports, but the ethical hacker must document their entire test. The ethical hacker takes more time to test the system, where a pen-tester takes very little time. The other major difference is that the ethical hacker must be certified in ethical hacking to determine vulnerabilities.

Reconnaissance

When ethically hacking, the first step is to gather information about the target of the hack. This is referred to as Reconnaissance. There are several methods to do this, and there is a wealth of information available on the internet about how to target a system. It is important to gather as much information about the target system as possible. There are several steps in reconnaissance. They include footprinting, enumeration, scanning networks, and vulnerability analysis. Examples of important information are:

- What is the target system

- What is the basic information about the target system

- What is the target's IP Address Ranges

- What are the target's DNS Records

- What are the Hostnames associated with the target

- What operating system is the target running

Reconnaissance is either active or passive. Active reconnaissance is when the hacker interacts with the computer system directly, while passive reconnaissance is discovering information about the target system from other sources. Passive reconnaissance is preferred to active, because active reconnaissance may be detected by the system administrator, who may take countermeasures against the hack.

An example of active reconnaissance is using port scanning to discover the ports of the target system.

An example of passive reconnaissance is running a whois search, which reveals a lot of information about the target website.

Footprinting

Footprinting is the accumulation of data about the target system. There are several tools and methods used in footprinting. These include web searches on various websites in addition to using the command line to gather public data on the system.

One of the easiest methods for footprinting is web searches. Some websites with public information about the target system are Netcraft, Linkedin, Google, and Whois.

Netcraft is a website that provides information about internet security. Searching for a web domain reveals the site, a status report, when the site was first seen, the netblock, and the operating system. Doing a search on Dell.com reveals the information that www.dell.com first appeared on the net on August 1995. It uses the netblock "akamai international, bv", and is running a Linux operating system.

Another website that reveals a large amount of data is monster.com. Monster is a job search website. It is useful because job recruiters often post very specific information on the technical aspects of the position being offered. The key requirements of the job listing generally reflect the technical information about the target system. For instance, a job might state that the employer is looking for an applicant with knowledge of Linux. This reveals that the target system is running Linux.

Linkedin.com is also an excellent source of information. Linkedin is a website where individuals post information about their previous or current employment and the skills they possess. If a person has skills in specific software, such as VMware Administration, and works for the company of the hack, it is safe to assume the target system uses VMware.

Google searches can also reveal a wealth of important information. A Google search of "apple.com ip address range" returns the following information from May 21, 2012:

The push service uses a load balancing scheme that yields a different IP address for the same hostname. However, the entire 17.0.0.0/8 address block is assigned to Apple so you can specify that range in your firewall rules. 17.0.0.0/**8** is a CIDR notation for 17.0.0.1 to 17.255.255.254.

This search revealed the IP block that Apple uses for its internal network.

Another useful tool is a whois search. A whois search can be done either through a web browser, or it can be done from the command line. A whois search reveals a wealth of information from name servers, email addresses, the name of the company, the company's physical address, and phone numbers. A whois search does not have to be a web domain, it can also be an IP address search. Knowing that Apple uses the entire 17.0.0.0/**8** IP address block, we can use a random IP from that block to run an additional search. This search yields the full Netrange, the domain registry, the organization's technical support's name, phone numbers, and email addresses. This is very useful in case the hack requires social engineering (see Chapter 4).

Network Scanning

Network scanning is scanning the network for open ports, hosts, data about the operating system, and the architecture of the network. There are three types of scanning. They are port scanning, network scanning, and vulnerability scanning.

- Port scanning is scanning that determines what ports are open or closed and what services the target system is running.

- Network scanning is a scan that detects IP addresses, OS details, Topography details, etc.

- Vulnerability scanning is a scan on the target system for vulnerabilities, specifically known vulnerabilities, and weaknesses.

The methodology of network scanning is to ping the system with an ICMP (Internet Control Message Protocol) echo request packet and wait for a ping reply, also called an ICMP echo reply. This reply contains information about the size of the packet and details of TTL (Time to Live). TTL is data used by DNS servers. The next step in the network scanning methodology is to scan for open ports, services being used, and the versions of those services. The best tool for port scanning is Nmap (see Chapter 10).

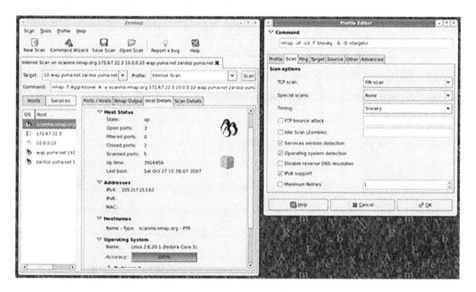

There are several types of scans. They are:

- TCP Connect Scan: In a TCP connection scan, a connection is made with the target server, which tells Nmap if the port is open or not with a connect system call.

- TCP Half-Open Scan: This scan, also called an SYN scan, attempts to locate open ports by attempting a three-way handshake, but only completing half of it. This scan attempts to establish a connection with every port on the server by sending an SYN packet. This is considered a stealthy scan and is generally preferable over a TCP connect scans.

- XMAS Scan: This scan, also referred to as a TCP scan, works by sending packets to the port. These packets can be PSH,

URG, or FIN flags. If the target ports send a reset response, then the ports are closed.

- FIN Scan: Like an XMAS scan, a FIN scan sends a FIN flag, and if there is no response the port is open.

- ACK Scan: An ACK scan does not determine if a port is open or closed. Instead, it determines if the port is protected by a firewall or another protection system.

- Null Scan: Null scanning is similar to XMAS scanning, except that it sends a packet with without TCP flags set.

- Idle Scan: An idle scan is a scan that takes advantage of the predictable IP ID flaw exploit without revealing the hacker's IP address.

Enumeration

Enumeration is the mathematical and computer science concept of listing all items in a set. The term is used in hacking to refer to checking all of the ports on a target system. Enumeration is the process of establishing a connection with the target system to perform queries to gain a basic knowledge of the network. Enumeration is essentially scanning ports to find information about the network. During enumeration, a hacker can extract information about file shares, usernames, group names, IP tables, hostnames, and other information. There are several types of protocols used in enumeration. The enumeration protocols are NetBIOS (Network Basic Input/Output System), SNMP (Simple Network Management Protocol), LDAP (Lightweight Directory Access Protocol), NTP (Network Time Protocol), SMTP (Simple Mail Transfer Protocol), DNS (Domain Name System), SMB (Server Message Block), and Linux/Windows. Enumeration is vital to hacking because the information gathered can be used in penetration attacks. Below is a list of Ports used in enumeration:

- TCP 53: DNS Zone transfer

- TCP 135: Microsoft RPC Endpoint Mapper

- TCP 137: NetBIOS Name Service

- TCP 139: NetBIOS session Service (SMB over NetBIOS)

- TCP 445: SMB over TCP (Direct Host)

- UDP 161: SNMP

- TCP/UDP 389: LDAP

- TCP/UDP 3368: Global Catalog Service

- TCP 25: Simple Mail Transfer Protocol (SMTP)

Vulnerability Analysis

The first step in vulnerability analysis is to classify and define the computer system and network resources. Next, determine the importance of the resources and the potential threats to the system. If threats are found, the next step for the ethical hacker is to create countermeasures. Vulnerability analysis is important for both the white and black hat hackers as it allows both to locate vulnerabilities that can be exploited.

The ethical hacker should include vulnerability analysis in their report to the company that hired them.

Chapter 4

Social, System, and IOT Hacks

Social Engineering

Social Engineering is an attempt by hackers to gain information about a target system from a legitimate authorized user. Social engineering takes advantage of end users general trust. Social engineering can take multiple forms such as hackers disguising themselves as legitimate employees or visitors, shoulder surfing, dumpster diving, befriending an employee on social media, and phishing attacks.

Hackers disguise themselves as genuine employees or visitors. Sometimes a hacker gains entry into a company building by following employees in, by making a fake ID, or disguising themselves as a legitimate visitor. Once inside the building, the hacker can engage in shoulder scanning. Shoulder scanning is when the hacker looks over the shoulder of end uses for usernames, passwords, and other important information about the network. Hackers might also look at whiteboards for proprietary information from presentations.

An example of this type of hack is a hacker goes to the company and claims to be a visitor. After gaining entry into the building, the hacker locates a system manual for the computer system and uses the information inside to mount an attack.

Another example is when the hacker calls an employee and claims to be a member of the IT team and asks the employee to either give information about the system or to make a change. This is often framed as a security check from the IT department. If the hacker determined the name of an IT member at the target organization, perhaps through footprinting, they could give that name, making them appear as a member of the IT team.

Another method is to dumpster dive. Companies often throw away important information into the garbage. This might include customer information, social security numbers, carbon copies from fax machines, and other useful information. Hackers climb into the company's dumpsters and go through the garbage looking for this information.

A highly effective method of social engineering is to befriend an employee over social media. By gaining the employee's trust, the hacker can gather information about the company including policies, the employee's username or password, computer system information, and how the system is protected. All of this information comes in handy for an attack. While ethical hackers rarely have the time to engage in this form of social engineering due to the time it takes to gain the employee's trust, the black hat can take weeks or months to gain this trust.

Sometimes a hacker does not have to engage with an employee directly to get information. Instead, the hacker can do a phishing attack. A phishing attack is when someone gets an email that appears legitimate that redirects to a fake website that asks for a username, password, or other personal information. If the target input this information, the hacker can use it in an attack. Phishing is a very common form of social engineering. Hackers also send fake emails with malware that infects computer systems.

System Hacking

System hacking is modifying hardware. By modifying hardware, a hacker can get the hardware to do something it was not designed for, reverse engineering software, or write new code for the hardware. The hacker may choose to hack devices that have known vulnerabilities. There are many tutorials and walkthroughs for modifying various devices on the web. Common devices that are hacked include mobile phones and tablet computers. System hacking usually voids any warranty the device might have.

A very basic hardware hack is overclocking the CPU or memory on the motherboard of a computer. CPUs run certain designed speeds and overclocking means that the hacker is changing the speed of the CPU or memory to make it faster. If a processor is overclocked too much, however, it might cause a heat issue and damage the motherboard.

Reverse engineering allows the hacker to analyze the code, which is often firmware, source code, or protocols. Modifying the software allows the hack to get the device to do something other what it was designed for or install malware on the device.

An example of modifying code on a device is iPhone jailbreaking. Jailbreaking is a term for modifying the restrictions built into the device by the manufacturer. In 2007 George Holz was the first hacker to jailbreak the iPhone. Holz went on to jailbreak the PlayStation 3. Jailbreaking tools for Apple products are readily available on the web. These tools have GUI interfaces, which makes them relatively easy to use. Jailbreaking tools give the hacker root access to iOS, Apple's mobile operating system; tvOS, Apple's OS for Apple TVs; and WatchOS, Apple's OS for the Apple Watch. Jailbreaking allows users to install applications that are not from the App Store, change carrier settings where the iPhone is usable on any cellular network, install malware, or customize the device.

IOT Hacking

IOT hacking is when the I/O on a device is altered. I/O stands for input/output, meaning any software or device that communicates data between a computer and another device. Basically, it means patching the software that controls the input or output of data being transferred between devices. Altering the I/O allows the hacker to add components to a device, such as extra buttons.

Replacing Components

Another type of hardware hacking is replacing components. By changing the electronics in a device, the hacker can change how the device operates or gives it additional functions than what the device was designed for. This includes changing or adding circuit boards or Circuit Bending. Circuit Bending is when a hacker changes components to alter sounds that the device makes.

Logic Analyzer

A logic analyzer is a device that is attached to a circuit board or chip. The device records signals on the electronics the device are sniffing. The data is sent to an analytical platform for a number crunch to see if the data is useful.

JTAG Hex Dump

JTag Hex Dump is a hack that reads, disassembles, and alters firmware. Firmware is the basic software that is programmed into the device's read-only memory. This is the software that runs the actual hardware of the device or machine.

Devices have ports that are used for programming the firmware. Hackers access these ports and read the hex-decimal software which allows hackers to transform the hex code into a programming language. The hacker alters the code, re-encodes the firmware into hex-decimal, and rewrites the device with the altered firmware. This process only works if the firmware is able to be flashed, or reset.

Chapter 5

What is that Smell?

Network Sniffing

Network sniffing is capturing data from a TCP/IP protocol. Network sniffing essentially is listening in on all the traffic on the network, and it can provide very useful information to the ethical hacker. Each device on a network has a different MAC (media access control) address that is wholly unique. Sniffing allows the hacker to listen in on all the conversations being sent back and forth on the TCP/IP network.

In Chapter 3, when discussing reconnaissance, there were two types, active and passive. Sniffing is passive and difficult to detect. Because sniffing is so hard to detect, a hacker can run it for long periods of time to map what kind of traffic is on the TCP/IP network. Sniffing can be done three different ways: internally, externally, or wirelessly. Sniffing can be software or hardware specifically designed for sniffing. An internal sniffer can detect all of the traffic on the network, where external sniffing provides information at the firewall level (see Chapter 7). Wireless sniffing allows the hacker to be physically close to the network and gain information over the wireless network.

System administrators use sniffing as well as hackers. Sniffing gives a list of the types of traffic on the network. For example, one form of sniffing shows how much VoIP (Voice over IP) traffic is happening on the network or how much web browsing is occurring.

Ethical usage for sniffing includes packet capturing, analysis of network traffic and usage, troubleshooting, or packet conversion for analysis. Unethical sniffing allows the hacker to identify users, steal passwords, steal data on email or message programs, data theft, and monetary damage. Hackers also use sniffing to build reputations for themselves.

LAN sniffing occurs when a sniffer is deployed on a LAN machine. This form of sniffing detects the entire IP range and is very difficult to detect. The information such a hack determines is what are the live hosts, server inventory, and open ports. This allows for port-specific attacks.

Protocol sniffing detects the protocols being used on the network. This process creates a list of protocols, which allows protocol specific sniffing, which is where an individual protocol is detected.

ARP sniffing intercepts data to make a map of Mac addresses and IP addresses. This is useful because it can lead to an ARP poisoning attack.

TCP session sniffing intercepts data traveling from a source to an IP address. If enough packets are sniffed, it gives the hacker information on service types, port numbers, and TCP sequences. This raw data is very useful to the hacker.

Application sniffing determines what applications are being used on the network. This form of sniffing allows for analysis of SQL queries, OS fingerprinting, and application-specific data. If the hacker has lists of applications, it is possible to perform application-specific attacks.

Web password sniffing uses HTTP sessions to steal data such as usernames and passwords. HTTP uses Secure Socket Layers (see Chapter 9) to secure the session, but internal websites often are less secure, with weaker encryption, which makes them easy targets for hackers.

Malware

According to a Google search, malware, or malicious software, is defined as "software that is intended to damage or disable computers and computer systems." Malware comes in many flavors including adware, spyware, ransomware, viruses, worms, trojans, backdoors, and rootkits. The majority of malware are trojan horses or viruses that infect computers, servers, or the web.

A trojan horse is a piece of code or software that appears to be a normal application but hides malicious code that damages the system or injects other malicious code such as ransomware or a virus.

Viruses, like trojan horses, appear as legitimate software or data, but they are self-replicating pieces of code designed to hog resources or destroy data. Many anti-virus programs detect and remove viruses from systems. Because of fact they self-replicate, viruses are an especially powerful form of attack.

Adware is software that displays ads on the system. The ads can overwhelm the computer's resources until it freezes the system. Adware can take a number of different forms. For instance, it can change a browser's homepage, display ads in a web browser, change search engine settings to a strange search engine, and pop-up ads on the screen. These pop-up ads will pop up so fast that a user cannot close the ads without even more ads popping up. This often continues until all of the system's resources are used up. The developer of the adware gets paid for the ads it displays.

Spyware is software that spies on a system or user. According to Google, spyware "enables a user to obtain covert information about another's computer activities by transmitting data covertly from their hard drive." An example of spyware is the keystroke logger. A keystroke logger is a software that records the keys pressed on the keyboard or the places touched on a touchscreen, as is the case of most mobile and tablet devices. Another example of spyware is a software that takes control of a computer's webcam to take pictures or video of the user or the user's home. This data can then be ransomed by the hacker.

Ransomware is software that denies the user access to the computer or threatens to spread personal information unless the person pays a ransom. Ransomware often uses worms or trojans to inject the ransomware code into the target system.

Backdoors are methods of intrusion where the software bypasses the encryption or authentication of a computer system. Backdoors are often installed to give hackers continual access to a machine or system. Backdoors are useful because they allow a hacker to continue to find vulnerabilities. Backdoors are often made by infecting the machine with a trojan or a worm.

Rootkits are software that gives an unauthorized user access or control of a computer, generally without detection by the system itself. Rootkits get their name because they seek root or administrator access to the system. Root access means the user can edit or delete any file on the computer system or server. Rootkits are very deadly because they can often modify the software used to detect them.

Chapter 6

Mother May I?

Denial of Service Attacks

A Denial of Service Attack (DoS) is a type of attack that prevents a legitimate user from being able to access a web server or computer system. This attack works by flooding the target system with requests that overwhelm it. A DoS attack uses one computer for the attack.

How a website or server typically works is that a computer makes a request of the webpage, the site or web server has a queue, and as a server responds to the request in the order, it received them in. As the server resolves the queue, it sends a reply. These requests might be for a specific page or multimedia on the site, but the requests sent by an attacking machine are not real requests. In a DoS attack, the attacking system makes a large number of requests very quickly. A large number of requests use up the web server's resources and clogs up the queue so that legitimate users cannot access the service. DoS attacks are very powerful. However, only one attacking computer is not going to take down a major website. One computer cannot create enough requests quickly enough to crash a major server.

There are several tools used for DoS attacks but the two most efficient are Slowloris and Low Orbit Ion Cannon (LOIC).

Slowloris runs in the terminal, using command line prompts, and it is the most powerful tool for DoS attacks. Slowloris runs on Peal programming language, so it is important to have Pearl installed before attempting to use Slowloris. If you are using Kali Linux, Slowloris is already installed by default.

To install Pearl use the following command line prompt in Terminal. Below is the code for installing Perl:

sudo apt-get install perl

sudo apt-get install libwww-mechanize-shell-perl

sudo apt-get install perl-mechanize

Once Pearl is installed, to launch a basic attack, first navigate to the extracted folder and run the command. Note that in the code below, replace < target.com > with an actual URL and delete the angle brackets.

chmod+x slowloris.pl

pearl slowloris.pl -dns < target.com >

The above basic attack is not very sophisticated and uses Slowloris' default settings. The following code is more advanced and is more likely to take down a webpage:

perl slowloris.pl -dns < target.com > -timeout 1 -num 1000 -cache

Another tool for DoS attacks is Low Orbit Ion Cannon. The difference between the two tools is that Slowloris runs in the terminal, while LOIC runs in a web browser and has a GUI (graphical user interface). Thus, instead of having to code on the command line, you have a user interface that makes attacks much easier. Because LOIC has a GUI, it is much easier to use for new ethical hackers. LOIC is downloadable for free from SorceForge, an online repository of free software.

Distributed Denial of Service Attacks

A Distributed Denial of Service (DDoS) attack uses the same process at a DoS attack, except that it uses a large number of computers, usually a botnet, instead of just one computer, to make the attack.

To perform a DDoS attack, the hacker must first build a botnet. This is done by using malware to take control of the target machines. Typically this attack is hidden from the legitimate user of the computer. A popular program for building botnets is ZueS.

Once the malware is distributed, and the botnet is created, the malware allows the hacker to take control over the all the zombie drones in the botnet with a Master Program. The botnet uses the zombie drones to mount an attack that uses the process as a DoS attack, except that it floods the server with requests from a large number of zombies. Because multiple computers are used, the frequency of the requests increases, which lengthens the queue, and makes it harder for a legitimate request to be completed. The botnet will continue to attack until the server crashes or the hacker defaces the website.

34

Chapter 7

Hand in the Honeypot

Evading IDS

To combat hackers, system administrators use intrusion detection systems (IDS). There are two types of IDS. The first is network-based IDS, and the other is host-based. Network IDS (NIDS) checks each packet in the network, looks for incorrect data or anomalies that might indicate an attack, raises alerts about hacked IPs or applications, and checks all traffic, generally by packet flittering. Host-based IDS include firewalls on the client machines.

These detection systems include physical firewalls, firewall software, and other IDS systems. IDS software filters packets and maintains Access Lists. This software is configured to check a packet's size, data, IP address, and other characteristics to pass and determine if the packet should be filtered. This is referred to as packet filtering.

There are several methods available to avoid IDS. They are:

- Stealth Scans: Stealth scanning is when an attacker uses NMAP or another port scanner to scan for open ports slowly, to not attract attention from the IDS.

- Packet Crafting: Packet crafting is when the attacker changes the size or the data inside a packet to evade IDS.

- War Dialing: War dialing is when an attacker detects modems to bypass IDS by attacking non-secured areas of the network.

35

- Decoy IP Addresses: Decoy IPs are when the attacker uses several proxy IPs so that there is a large number of packets from different IP addresses, which increases the chance of getting packets past the filters.

- Idle Zombie Scans: Idle zombie scanning is when the attacker creates a bot or botnet and uses them to attempt to bypass the IDS.

- Randomize: This attack is when the attacker randomizes the number, size, or the data inside the packets to evade the IDS.

Honeypots

Honeypots are traps that system administers set-up to trap and track attackers. Honeypots are kept separate from the rest of the network and are filled with false data that appears real and very attractive to the attacker. Honeypots are generally out of date systems placed strategically on the network with very low security, including a generic username and password. Honeypots will also have open ports, so they are easy to locate. Honeypots can be installed on a physical machine, or a computer can run multiple virtual honeypots, each appearing to be a physical computer on the network with valuable data. When the attacker gains access to the honeypot, the IDS begins tracking and logging the attacker. Triggering the honeypot causes the IDS to deny privileges on the network to the attacker. A large reason why honeypots are useful is that they can detect zero-day malware that is not yet included in anti-malware software.

Chapter 8

Hacking the Web

Web Applications

As more devices that use web applications are released onto the market, such as mobile phones, tablets, and computers, hacking web applications has become more prevalent as there are more and more web applications available, each with its own bugs, exploits, and vulnerabilities. Hacking web applications becomes easier every day as hackers discover new exploits in web applications. Below are some forms of web application attacks.

Session Hijacking

Session Hijacking is a type of cyber attack where the attacker exploits a web server's session tokens. The hacker does this by exploiting a control mechanism, which controls the session tokens.

Web servers must communicate with several different TCP connections. The server needs to keep track of the connections, so it issues a session token after the computer or device is authenticated. This token can be used in cookies, the header of an http request, or in the body of the header requisition.

A session hijacking attacks the session token by predicting a token or by stealing one. Once the hacker compromises the session token it can exploit the following:

One kind of attack predicts the ID values and allows the hacker to get into a system without authentication.

A session sniffing attack happens when a user sends a request with a session ID to the web server, and the hacker intercepts the session ID and uses it to create their own requests on the web server, effectively hiding the attacker as a user.

A client-side attack is a type of attack that exploits the vulnerabilities in software clients such as web browsers, pdf reader/writers, instant messengers, and other software with vulnerabilities. IBM's Knowledge Center (www.ibm.com/support/knowledgecenter/en) lists two types of client-side attacks. They are content spoofing and Cross-site scripting (XSS). Content spoofing is when a user thinks that the content on the site is valid and legitimate and not originating from external sources. XXS is when an attacker executes scripts in a browser. According to IBM, "This attack is used to intercept user sessions, deface websites, insert hostile content, conduct phishing attacks, and take over the user's browser by using scripting malware."

A Man-in-the-middle attack (MITM) occurs when a hacker intercepts an http transaction. The attacker takes the TCP connection and splits it in two, allowing the attacker to read, function as a proxy, or modify the data in the message. A popular tool for MITM attacks is Ettercap.

- Man-in-the-browser attacks are similar to MITM attacks, except they use a trojan horse to attack banking information like transactions and balances.

SQL Injection

SQL injection is when an attacker adds SQL queries into an input form on an application. The SQL statements are executed and allow the attacker to read sensitive data from a database, have admin access allowing it to shut down, modify the database, recover content in a file in the database, and issue commands to the OS. SQL injection is often used on financial data such as changing balances or voiding transactions. It also allows the attacker to spoof identity, disclose all of the data in the database, destroy data, or gain administer privileges of the database.

Cross-Site Scripting (XXS)

There are three types of XXS attacks: Stored or non-persistent XXS, Reflected or persistent XXS; and DOM-based XXS.

- Stored XXS attacks happen when a user's input is saved on a web server. This attack often occurs in a database, on forums, or in comments sections of a website.

- Reflected XXS occurs when a message is returned from the web server with an error message or a search result that is sent to the client.

- DOM-based XXS occurs when the data is in DOM, and the data does not leave the browser. DOM stands for Document Object Model and is an HTML and XML interface for documents.

Wireless Networking

Wireless networks are a set of multiple devices that communicate over radio waves within a certain range. Wireless networks let multiple devices connect to the internet via a modem and a wireless router. The router controls the settings of the wireless network including IP addresses, MAC addresses, the wireless network's authentication, and other settings. Wireless routers use IEEE 802.11, which is a set of MAC addresses and physical layer settings. Attacks on wireless networks are generally sniffing attacks that attempt to obtain the SSID and gain access to the wireless network.

Wireless DoS attacks

Wireless networks are susceptible to two types of attacks. The first is physical attacks, and it occurs when there is radio interference from cordless phones. The second type of attack is a network DoS attack. A network DoS attack is easy to accomplish. Like other DoS attacks, it operates by sending multiple requests, in this instance to an Access Point. Because the requests are taking up resources and clogging the queue, legitimate devices cannot connect to the network with their requests.

Mobile Platforms

The majority of attacks on mobile platforms come in the form of malware for the different mobile platforms. The major mobile platforms are Android and iOS. Android is a mobile platform, and since Android devices have a large market share, there is a large number of devices to attack. Not all malware is installed via an app store, however, some malware attacks via a QR (Quick Response) code. Hacking mobile devices provide a wealth of information about the user. Hackers can access contacts, GPS data, the microphone, the camera, emails, MMS messages, and SMS messages.

Android

Android was developed by Google and is available as an open-source mobile platform. The majority of the malware written for mobile devices is for Android because it there are more avenues to attack it. The Android OS allows users to add software from third-party application stores as well as the official Google Play store. Malicious apps can come from either source, as Google does not put their apps through as strict a vetting process. The software on Android phones is susceptible to reverse-engineering, which increases the danger inherent in the platform. Also, a large number of Android phones do not come encrypted, making malware attacks easier to perform. Adware is popular malware for Android devices.

AndroidVulnerabilities.org lists several exploits that fall into the categories of kernel, network, signature, and system vulnerabilities.

Apple

Apple developed three mobile platforms iOS, tvOS, and watchOS. They are operating systems for iPhones, iPads, Apple TVs, and Apple Watches. There are fewer malware attacks on the Apple products due to the higher level of security and because the App Store is monitored heavily and it is hard to get malicious apps onto the App Store for any length of time. The Apple Mobile OSs does not allow for silent SMS which makes it is more difficult to spread malicious software.

Web Servers

A web server is the computer, hardware, and software that stores information on a web service, and makes that information available either over LAN or the internet. Web servers hold large amounts of sensitive data such as social security numbers, credit card numbers, email addresses, and passwords. An example of a famous attack on a web server is the Equifax hack in 2017. The hack exposed the personal data of millions of people including information about the victims' credit. Hacking a web server is a complex attack.

Web servers have several vulnerabilities. These vulnerabilities include using default settings, the web server is misconfigured, exploiting bugs, or there is simply a lack of security. The types of web servers are:

- Apache: Apache web servers are the most commonly used. Apache typically is run on Linux.

- Internet Information Services (IIS): IIS is a web server for Windows. It is the second most used, after Apache.

- Other: There are other web servers on the market including Novell's web server and Mac OS X server.

Types of Attacks

There are several types of attacks a hacker can use to crack a web server. These types of attacks include directory traversable attacks, DoS and DDoS attacks, domain name system hacking, sniffing, phishing, pharming, and defacement. Domain name system hacking is when an attacker changes the Domain Name System (DNS) settings so that the internet traffic for the web server is instead sent to the hacker's web server. A pharming attack is when the attacker changes the DNS settings on the user's computer. There are defacement attacks, which is when the attacker replaces a website's webpage with another one that including the hacker's name and whatever media the hacker chooses to post. Defacement is often done to build a hacker's reputation.

Chapter 9

Hacking the Cloud

Cloud Computing Security

Cloud computing cryptography is the security used by cloud services. It is a combination of cryptography and encryption that attempts to protect user's data. The cloud offers great flexibility in terms of processing power, storage, and services with relatively easy access from many users. Users can access cloud computing servers to log into virtual machines with all of the resources saved on a server rather than running on the computer itself.

Security for cloud computing is very poor. The user is subject to the security of the service, which is unique to the various services and generally not very secure. Cloud computing suffers from several security vulnerabilities including database misconfigurations. The benefits of targeting the cloud are that it reveals information about commerce, which the hacker can use for financial gain. Cloud computing is vulnerable to information leakage. Information leakage is when an attacker gains access to a system designed to close to the public, but an attacker is able to gain information from the system. Cloud computing also suffers from being an open environment, which means that vulnerabilities are system-wide.

RedLock, a computer security company, which detected the 2018 cryptojacking of Tesla, vice president Upa Cambell said:

The benefit of the cloud is agility, but the downside is that the chance of user error is higher. Organizations are really struggling.

Types of Cloud Computing

There are two types of cloud computing. The first is the services offered and the second is what type of cloud is it.

The following are types of types of clouds based on their location:

- Public Cloud: A public cloud is open to public use, and the system is hosted by the service provider and is stored at their premises.

- Private Cloud: Private clouds are computing infrastructures for specific organizations, and the resources are not shared outside the organization.

- Hybrid Cloud: Hybrid clouds are clouds that offer both private and public computing infrastructure. Critical processes are on a private cloud while applications are run on a public club.

- Community Cloud: Community clouds are shared by multiple organizations.

The second type of cloud computing is by types of services the cloud offers. Below are the types of services:

- Infrastructures as a Service: Infrastructures as a service (IaaS) is when the service offers virtual machines, operating systems, and abstracted hardware are stored on the cloud.

- Platform as a Service: Platform as a service (PaaS) is when the cloud computing vendor offers a development platform. Platforms from vendor to vendor are not compatible.

- Software as a Service: Software as a service (SaaS) os when the entire software is offered on the cloud, which allows on-demand use.

Cloud Computing Cryptography

Cryptography itself is the process of converting text from plain text into a cipher that the receiver then converts back into plain text. The process varies depending on if the cryptography that is used for a public key infrastructure (PKY) or Secure Socket Layer (SSL). Below are details on the two types of encryption.

Public Key Infrastructure

Public Key Infrastructure is a set of policies, procedures, and roles that are used to create, distribute, revoke, store, use, and manages digital certificates. It also manages public key encryption.

To get a digital certificate the user sends the public encryption key to the registration authority to the verifier, which sends the key to verification, who uses the public and private keys to verify the user. It then hands the key to the certificate authority who issues the certificate with a digital signature and an expiration date.

Secure Socket Layer

Secure Socket Layer is a cryptosystem with a public key used over the application layer to encrypt the data in HTTP. SSL changes the size of blocks of incoming data by fragmenting them, encrypting them, compressing them, and adding a MAC header before transferring it to the receiving end. There are four protocols in SSL. They are:

- Handshake: A handshake protocol establishes the connection.

- Cipher-Spec: A cipher-spec protocol is used to end the handshake.

- Record: A record protocol carries data.

- Alert: The alert protocol is used for any notifications.

Cryptojacking

Cryptojacking is a new kind of attack where the hacker attacks a cloud computer, creates a mining server and begins to mine cryptocurrency. While cryptocurrency uses a large amount of processor power and electricity which is usually easy to notice, yet on a cloud computer the service already uses a large amount of processor power and electricity. The attacker often goes unnoticed. To maintain the mining server, the attacker uses an unusual IP port to hide it from port scanners. The mining server works in the background, mining cryptocurrency that can be sold for a large profit.

Chapter 10

Tools

An ethical hacker needs several tools to effectively hack computer systems. Below is a list of the various tools necessary for ethical hacking.

Burp Suite

Burp Suite is a tool for penetration testing. Burp has an up-to-date database of vulnerabilities for web applications. Burp is written in Java, so it is usable on any system including Windows, Mac OS X, Linux, and Unix operating systems. Burp is designed to do penetration testing by running actual attacks on web applications, which makes the tool useful to both system administrators and hackers. The Burp software package includes following functionality:

- HTTP Proxy: This function allows Burp to operate as a proxy server, which allows it to intercept, inspect, and modify raw data. This function allows Burp to make man-in-the-middle attacks.

- Scanner: The scanner functions as a security scanner for web applications.

- Intruder: The intruder function allows Burp to make automated attacks against web applications.

- Spider: The spider operates as a web crawler. A web crawler is a piece of software or code that searches through web pages and creates an index of the data. This process allows the spider to mine data from web pages.

47

- Repeater: The repeater tool is used to modify requests, send requests, and analyze the data from requests.

- Decoder: The decoder tool transforms raw data into coding language, and vice versa.

- Comparer: The comparer tool compares two items of data.

- Extender: The extender tool allows Burp users to add functions to the program.

- Sequencer: The sequencer is a tool that checks the randomness in a data sample.

Ettercap

Ettercap is a network security tool that allows hackers to make man-in-the-middle attacks. Ettercap runs on a variety of operating systems including Windows, Linux, Mac OS X, Solaris and other operating systems. Ettercap operates by using ARP poisoning against target computers.

- Ettercap has four features that come built into it, but the software allows the user to add additional features. The basic four features are:

- IP-based: In this mode, Ettercap filters the packets based on the IP source and destination.

- Mac-based: In this mode, Ettercap filters the packets based on Mac addresses. This method is good for sniffing through a gateway.

- ARP-based: In this mode, Ettercap uses ARP poisoning to sniff LAN computers between two hosts. This is also called a full-duplex.

- PublicARP-based: In this mode, Ettercap uses ARP poisoning to sniff LAN connections from a victim host to other hosts. This is called a half-duplex.

ICE IV

ICE IV or ICE 9 is a software that creates botnets. It is based on the ZueS code, which holds the records for the number of zombie drones a botnet has created. Ice IV creates botnets by sending out trojan horses that install malware on the zombie, allowing the hacker to take control of it.

John the Ripper

John the Ripper is a Linux-based password cracker. John the ripper is included in both the Kali Linux distribution and is packaged with the Metasploit framework.

Jxplorer

Jxplorer is an LDAP browser and editor. According to the JXplorer website, Jxplorer "is a compliant general purpose LDAP client that can be used to search, read and edit any standard LDAP directory, or any directory service with an LDAP or DSML interface."

Kali Linux

Kali Linux is a Debian-derived Linux distribution that is designed for network security and white hat hacking. Kali Linux describes itself as a "penetration and ethical hacking Linux Distribution." Kali includes many of the hacking tools in the initial software installation of the OS.

As a Linux system, it has easy access to the Command Line. Several of the tools included in Kali are also discussed in this chapter.

Some of the tools included in Kali Linux are:

- Aircrack-ng

- Burp Suite

- Cisco Global Exploiter

- Ettercap

- John the Ripper

- Kismet

- Maltego

- Metasploit framework

- Nmap

- OWASP ZAP

- Wireshark

- DVWA

Kismet

- Kismet is wireless network detector that works without sending packets. It is able to monitor wireless clients and wireless access points. The tool also allows sniffing. Kismet has the following features:

- Sniffing of media access controls.

- PCAP logging.

- Modular architecture.

- Plug-in architecture to add new features.

- Capture multiple source support.

- Ability to export packets to other tools.

- Remote sniffing and remote capture.

- XML output for use in other tools.

Low Orbit Ion Cannon

Low Orbit Ion Cannon (LOIC) is a DoS tool. LOIC sends a multitude of requests to a website or server to flood it with requests so that legitimate users cannot use the webpage or server. LOIC can run on Windows, Mac (using Wine), or Linux.

Maltego

Maltego is an information gathering tool used for forensics and penetration testing. Maltego picks up a lot of information when scanning a domain. Maltego is extremely useful because it puts the data into charts and graphs similar to those used by Data Scientists. In a scan, Maltego can determine:

- People's names, email addresses, and aliases

- Social Networks

- Companies

- Organizations

- Websites

- Affiliations

- Documents and files

- Internet infrastructure including domains, Netblocks, IP addresses, and DNS names

Metasploit

Metasploit is an exploitation framework of tools for the creation of exploits and system administration. There are free open-source and commercial versions of Metasploit available. According to Metasploit's website the software "provides the infrastructure, content, and tools to perform penetration tests and extensive security auditing." A plus to Metasploit is that it is open-source with many developers work on it and new exploits being added on a regular basis, keeping the software current. Metasploit is useful during many phases of hacking including penetration testing. Metsploit includes dozens of tools.

nbtstat

nbstat is a Microsoft created Windows tool that reviews packets with NetBIOS over TCP/IP.

Netcraft

Netcraft is a website that gives information about a domain and its activities. This tool is used in footprinting.

NetScanTools Pro

NetScanTools Pro, also called simply NetScan, is a Windows-based software that is used for network troubleshooting and information gathering about a network. According to netscantools.com, NetScanTools "research IPv4 addresses, IPv6 addresses, hostnames, domain names, email addresses, and URLs automatically or with manual tools." NetScan is a tool often used in the enumeration to scan for open ports.

Nmap

Nmap is used for port scanning, to discover services on a network, or for mapping a network. Nmap essentially works by sending packets and analyzing the responses. It is an open-source tool that is available on Nmap's website.

Nmap features include:

- Host Discovery: Discovering hosts on a computer network

- Port Scanning: Enumerating open and closed ports by attempting 3-way handshakes

- Version Detection: Determining the name and versions of applications on a network

- OS Detection: Determining the hardware and operating systems of network devices

- Interaction with the target via scripts: Sending scripts to the target computer system or network

- OpUtils Network Monitoring Toolset

- OpUtils Network Monitoring Toolset is a software tool for switching port and IP addresses. OpUtils is a paid-for tool that is available online.

Slowloris

Slowloris is the most effective software for making Denial of Service (see Chapter 6) attacks. Slowloris is a software that runs on command line prompts, and it follows a similar scripting structure as the command line. Hence, some experience with the command line is preferable before attempting to use this tool.

- **Superscan**

- Superscan is a port scanning software that detects TCP and UDP ports on a computer system. Superscan is a free tool.

- **Wireshark**

- Wireshark is a network protocol analyses. It is used to track the traffic on a network. This analysis can be done for either a wired or wireless network.

- Wireshark Features Include:

- Deep inspection of hundreds of protocols

- Multi-Platform: Runs on Windows, Linux, macOS, and other operating systems

- Network data is displayed in a GUI or by the TTY-mode TShark utility

- VoIP analysis

- Ability to read and write many file formats

- Captures files archived with gzip

- Decryption support for protocols

- Display's live data from Ethernet, IEEE 802.11, ATM, and other systems

Conclusion

Thank for making it through to the end of *Ethical Hacking: A Comprehensive Beginner's Guide to Learn and Master Ethical Hacking*, let's hope it was informative and able to provide you with all of the tools you need to achieve your goals, whatever they may be. Now that you have finished this book, the opportunities are endless, but there is still much to learn. Keep reading and learning more about ethical hacking to broaden your perspective. It is the only way to master the skills you need to be an ethical hacker.

The next step is to stop reading, download the tools, and get started hacking to learn more and master the skills you need, no matter if you are seeking your ethical hacking certification, want to learn more about the techniques you just learned, or are to just out to have some fun. Use the skills you have learned to gain a reputation as an ethical hacker and impress your friends and colleagues with your newfound talents.

Complex tasks are easiest to learn when they are broken down into manageable sizes, and hacking is no exception. Breaking down the skills, methods, and tools you need is important. Setting individual deadlines will help you achieve your goals. It is important to set your own deadlines to keep yourself on task and moving forward.

Finally, if you found this book useful in any way, a review on Amazon is always appreciated!